THE EASTERN PATH TO HEAVEN

THE EASTERN PATH TO HEAVEN

A Guide to Happiness from the Teachings of Jesus in Tibet

GESHE MICHAEL ROACH
AND LAMA CHRISTIE MCNALLY

SEABURY BOOKS
New York

Library of Congress Cataloging-in-Publication Data

Roach, Michael, 1952-
The Eastern path to heaven : a guide to happiness from the teachings of Jesus in Tibet / by Michael Roach and Christie McNally.
p. cm.
ISBN 978-1-59627-097-8 (pbk.)
1. Jesus Christ – Buddhist interpretations. 2. Christianity and other religions – Buddhism. 3. Buddhism – Relations – Christianity. I. McNally, Christie. II. Title.
BT304.914.R63 2008
261.2′43 – dc22

2007048881

Church Publishing Incorporated
445 Fifth Avenue
New York, NY 10016
www.churchpublishing.org

5 4 3 2 1

May everyone who searches
Find their own true path
To Heaven

Contents

Two
SECURITY

Three
LOVE

1

The Courage to Have It All

Jesus said,

> *Ask, and it shall be given to you;*
> *Seek, and ye shall find;*
> *Knock, and it shall be opened unto you.*

Let us have the courage to get everything we want from this life.

We have tried like children to make ourselves happy. And we have failed.

Too early we have given up hoping that we can have everything.

If someone came and showed us a way to have it all, it is not that we would be afraid to follow this way. What frightens us is the very idea of having everything come true.

So first, let us have the courage.

2

What Is It All?

Jesus said,

All things are possible.

No one needs to tell us what would make us happy. We know it from our birth. We know we did not come into this world to eat and work and die.

We have a right to be healthy and strong. We have a right to have all the things we need. We have a right to find love.

And we have higher rights. We have a right to be happy, all day, every day. We have a right to free ourselves from the fear of death. We have a right to fulfill our true destiny: it is our right to become someone who can take care of every other person in the world.

Let us take what is ours, by right.

3

A Star in the East

After the death of Jesus, the disciples gathered together in Jerusalem—

> *And there appeared unto them forked tongues of light like fire, that came and sat upon them, and they began to speak in all the different languages of the world.*

Thus did Christ begin the mission of the apostles. Peter was sent west. He laid the foundation for the great churches around us; his deeds are written in stone.

Thomas, though, was sent by Jesus east along the routes of trade and ideas paved by Alexander the Great across Persia to India. Time and war have erased his footprints, tracks in melted snow.

But the wisdom of Thomas reached even the mountains of Tibet, where it nestled protected for thousands of years.

Every disciple and country and language has preserved for us different sides of Jesus. The long-lost eastern branch of our Christian family can show us what we already have.

ONE

STRENGTH

4

The One Key of Christ

Jesus said,

There is no one among you
Who shall not receive
A hundred times more now,
And life without end
In the time to come.

And so we begin, with something small and worldly. Teach me how to stay healthy, strong, and beautiful.

Because if there is a key to the universe, it should work for both our immediate needs and for our eternal needs as well.

Which is to say, perhaps this world and the world beyond are found in the very same place. Perhaps it is by perfecting my small world now that the eternal world then comes.

Let us have the courage to see that eternal happiness begins by making our happiness here.

5

The True Image

On the Mount, God gave Moses the Ten Commandments, and among the first of them was—

Thou shalt not make unto thee any graven image.

But what does it mean? And why is it so important for us?

On the one hand, we are simply incapable of sculpting an image of the divine. Any attempt we make will be imperfect and misleading. A child drawing its parent's face.

But images are imperfect in a deeper way too. When different people look at a single thing, we all see something slightly different.

So where is the real thing? What is God's true image? Perhaps it's simply that no image we can create is the one. Perhaps this itself is the one true image.

Be patient. These are things we need to know. If there is one key to the universe, it must be something we haven't thought of before.

6

First Came the Word

The first words of the Gospel of John say:

In the beginning was the Word.

Why do all of us see different things when we look at a single thing?

I look at a painting and see something beautiful. You look at the same painting and see something ugly. This proves that the beauty I see cannot be coming from the painting.

So it must be coming from me.

We saw our first car, and Mother taught us the word for it, "car."

But you *saw* a car before you knew its name. You knew where its edges started and stopped. And so somehow it was already inside of you. A picture in the mind: the true word for "car." And this word came first.

Maybe the way my own body looks and feels is coming from . . . me.

7

How the Word Began

Jesus said,

> *I swear to you, that one day*
> *You will give an accounting*
> *Of every word you have ever spoken.*

Word-pictures emerge from our hearts and decide how we see the world. But who put them in our minds in the first place?

We have a working memory which allows us to remember to pick up something at the market on the way home from work.

And we have a deeper memory which records every single thing we have ever done or said or thought over our entire lifetime.

I am walking on the grass. A butterfly lands at my feet. I step aside so I won't crush it.

This one kindness enters my deeper memory. It stays there and slowly becomes a word, a picture. And then the picture emerges, as the beauty of a painting.

8

Do unto Others

Jesus said,

> *Do unto others*
> *As you would have them do*
> *Unto you.*

And so the beauty inside a painting is coming from a picture or seed that I planted in my own mind when I did something kind to others.

If I want a beautiful life, or a strong and healthy body, then all I need to do is plant the right seeds inside my own mind.

By doing the same to others.

Let us have the courage to see the truth: we can have only what we give to others.

9

My Brother's Keeper

Cain asked the Lord,

Am I my brother's keeper?

Is there any real reason why I should take care of others with the same effort that I take care of myself?

If this idea about our deeper memory is correct, then paying attention to what other people need is simply the most intelligent thing we can do.

If you are sick and I stop my busy life to care for you, then I have contributed to your health. As I watch myself take care of you, new seeds are planted within my deep memory. They turn into word-pictures and emerge, and I experience my own body as stronger.

When I decide to be my brother's keeper, I am keeping both of us.

10

Thou Shalt Not Kill

God said, and Jesus repeated,

Thou shalt not kill.

And so because of the deeper memory, we are doing to ourselves whatever we do to others.

We said that our first right in this life is to a strong and healthy body. If my body is getting old, if I have some sickness, or if I only want to be more trim or attractive or have more energy, then the only way is to protect the lives and health of those around me.

Why does aspirin work for one person and not for another? Why does exercise make one person strong and injure another?

The beauty in the painting is coming from me. And so we must go and master the art of protecting the lives of others.

11

The Least of My Commandments

Jesus said,

> *Ye have heard that it was said by them of olden times, "Thou shalt not kill." But I say unto you that anyone who is only angry with their brother is in great danger.*

Jesus is telling us that we must never kill, for in killing others we damage our own bodies as surely as we do theirs.

And in our minds we answer "But I have not killed others, and still I have some sickness. Still my energy diminishes, year by year."

And Jesus replies, it is not enough, it is not enough. It is not enough simply not to kill. We must protect life; we must honor life.

We must examine our lives constantly and root out any small thing we do that may hurt someone else. A moment's careless driving, a pen left on the floor. A single thought of anger that could lead to something more.

12

War Doesn't Work

Jesus said,

> *If someone comes and strikes you on the right cheek, then turn to them the other cheek, so they can strike you there as well.*

The idea that our world may be coming from ourselves — from what we do to others — throws doubt upon all our ideas of how to respond to violence.

If someone at home or at work or halfway around the world does something to hurt me, this is really just a picture from my own deep memory — an echo of some harm I myself did to someone else in the past.

If I respond now by hurting the person back, I plant a new seed to see myself hurt again; it might emerge, for example, as a bad back.

Turning the other cheek, refusing to hurt those who hurt us, is not just the right thing to do. It's the most intelligent thing to do.

In fact, that's what *makes* it right.

13

Wisdom for Our Choices

Jesus said,

> *Inasmuch as ye have done it unto the least of these, ye have done it unto me.*

As might be expected, some of the teachings of Jesus are much clearer as they have survived within the wisdom of India and Tibet.

In these traditions, it is stated that if we hope for any strength and health ourselves, we must protect the life of both those who are already born and those who are not yet born. Life and consciousness, all these teachings say, begin at the very moment of conception, when the sperm meets the egg.

It is good to be aware of how Christ's words went east, in making choices that affect others, and thus ourselves.

14

A Single Sparrow

Jesus said,

Not a single sparrow
Is forgotten
before God.

Animals can be one of the greatest sources of comfort in our lives. A happy dog wagging its tail, a cat purring in our lap — these are simple joys. We know our pets feel things, because it feels so good to make them feel good.

And so in honoring life we must honor the lives of all creatures — even those who are much smaller than we are, or those who cannot speak like us. After all, this applies to human babies as well!

There are times — for example, as we drive a car — when perhaps we cannot avoid harming the lives of animals. But it is a different matter to kill them purposely, or even for sport. These we can choose not to do.

15

Beauty

It's one thing to have a body full of energy and strength. But we can also plant seeds in the deep memory that will actually make us more attractive.

There's nothing wrong with beauty. The point of this whole process is that, in the end, we gain the exquisite body of an angel. But we're getting ahead of ourselves.

The seed for beauty is planted by the single act of not getting angry at times when anyone would want to get angry. Peter said unto the Lord,

> *How often should my brother hurt me, and I forgive him? Up to seven times?*

And Jesus replied,

> *I say not unto thee, up to seven times, but rather seventy times seven.*

16

The Art of Eating

We constantly see Jesus deciding to fast in order to sharpen his prayers. Oftentimes he simply forgets to eat.

Many of us who live in countries where there is plenty of food find ourselves unable to control our appetites. The simple act of eating, which is meant to strengthen our body, has become for many of us a danger to our health and life.

There's an easy way to control ourselves around food. We use what we've learned about deep memory.

Whenever we have a chance to help someone *else* eat more wisely, we take it, quietly. If friends come over to visit, we offer them something healthy to eat.

Serving those around us this way comes back to us, and we simply don't feel like eating too much, or eating things that are not healthy for us.

◆ ◆ ◆

Understanding thus the words of Jesus in a new light, in the light of his teachings that went eastward from the cross, we can regain our health and youthful strength and appearance. With our new, strong body we go next and fulfill our right to security: to having the things we want and need.

TWO

SECURITY

17

My Only Lord and Master

We've been talking about jewels from the teachings of Christ that lie hidden in the teachings of the East. It's easier to accept and use this wisdom ourselves if we know more about its history.

The beginning of the story is also a most important lesson. Here then is how the disciple Thomas was sent to India, from an ancient Syriac manuscript called the *Acts of Thomas*.

As we know, Jesus appeared to his disciples a number of times after his death in order to give them instructions on how to continue their mission.

At one of these gatherings, he had the disciples write down the names of different countries on slips of paper.

Each disciple then closed his eyes and chose a country from a bowl.

Thomas pulled out India but flatly refused to go. After all, even the armies of Alexander the Great had turned back after conquering India, since everyone knew it was the end of the world, and after that you could only fall off. Who wants to get stuck out at the end of the world?

Jesus appeared one night in Thomas's own room to speak to him alone, urging him to accept his assignment. But Thomas steadfastly refused, saying he was a simple Jew who knew nothing about India or its people. It would be useless for him to go.

During the day Jesus went to the marketplace, there in Jerusalem. He approached a man named Habban, whose business was buying and selling slaves, a legal and very common occupation in the times of our Lord.

Habban specialized in the exotic, on an international scale. He traveled to India dragging along skilled craftsmen of many lands, men who might have gotten in debt, because bankruptcy in those days meant finally having to sell yourself as a slave to someone else.

The wealthy in India wanted houses and artwork done in the Greek way, for by Christ's time kings from Greece had ruled over parts of India for hundreds of years. They brought changes in the customs and styles and ways of thinking of these lands, unknowingly preparing the way for people like Thomas.

On the way back from India, Habban would bring what were delicately called "dancing girls," for sale in Jerusalem.

Now on this particular day, Habban happened to have an order from an elderly Indian king who needed an architect and builder who could design and direct the construction of a palace, in both stone and timber — a skill that Thomas just happened to have.

And so Jesus appeared out of the crowd and offered to sell his slave Thomas to Habban, to be locked in chains and carted off to the world's end.

Habban was suspicious. The deal seemed too good, because Jesus was asking for only twenty pieces of silver — which was ten pieces less than the cost of a common household slave. But Jesus knew that a disciple could not fetch more than his teacher had already. Habban demanded that the deal be put in writing — and Jesus just happened to have a bill of sale already prepared and waiting.

Get this picture: Thomas is strolling down one of the winding streets of Jerusalem, in the fine weather just after the first Easter.

Habban is still balking: "I'll buy the man if we go to him together and if he admits in front of us both that you are his rightful owner."

Jesus points to Thomas, walking up the street. Habban runs and takes the startled disciple by the arm.

Habban gestures to Jesus: "Is this man your master?"

Thomas looks up in adoration and answers, "Yes, yes, my only Lord and Master."

◆ ◆ ◆

Thomas was taken in chains and sold to the aging Indian king. He never returned home, but died on a hill along the eastern coast of India.

Thomas's teachings spread throughout the Middle East and Asia. His own account of what Christ taught, the *Gospel of Thomas*, is one of Christianity's most important books. It was unearthed in 1945 at Nag Hammadi in Egypt, not far from the shipping route that led Thomas and Habban across the Red Sea and on to India.

18

A Living Teacher

The story of Thomas is a crucial one for us. We can read through a small book like this, or even the entire New Testament, in a matter of days. We can understand it and embrace it heartily, but then the real work begins.

How do we translate these new ideas into our lives? How do we make them a regular part of every day? Because otherwise we can never plant enough seeds to see things change in a big way.

The first thing we need now is a living teacher. Someone who pushes us beyond the limits of our own courage and vision. Someone who's willing to drag us there in chains if that's what it takes. Someone we can talk to and ask our questions. Someone who's been through it already. Someone we can trust. A living link in a chain that goes all the way back to the living Lord.

19

Ye Shall Receive

Jesus said—

Give, and ye shall receive.

It's a goodness to be healthy and strong. After we reach that, we need the basic kinds of security: a good income, a good home, and the things we need to live comfortably. Sensible needs that provide a foundation for a life led in goodness.

Again the principle is overwhelmingly simple. First we make a list of what we would like to achieve physically: a certain income, a meaningful job, such-and-such a place to live.

Then we go about seeing that others get these things first.

Every little action we take to provide for others is recorded in our deep memory. There it evolves into a word-picture and emerges as that pretty little house we always dreamed of.

20

They Do Not Prosper

Jeremiah asked the Lord,

Why do the wicked prosper?

Some very obvious questions should be popping up in your mind right now. Perhaps they popped up first when you were a child. The teachings of Christ as they went east with Thomas can be a tremendous help here.

So, first, we see people who are generous to others and still fail to succeed financially in their job or business. We see others who refuse to share or perhaps even cheat people but who nonetheless get rich.

Seeds planted in a field take time to grow. So do those we plant in our deep memory. People who succeed in September planted good seeds in August, or earlier.

And whatever negative seeds they are planting now *must* come back to them later. This is a truth that cannot fail, for good or for bad. Let us not be misled by appearances.

21

Speeding Things Up

Jesus said,

> *I tell you of a truth, that there are some of you standing here who shall not taste of death before they see the kingdom of God.*

It's not very comforting for someone to tell us that bad people who are successful now must have done something good before, and that they will suffer later on. It's almost impossible for us to act on some vague promises that whatever good we do now will be rewarded later, perhaps not even until after we die.

In the powerful words above, Jesus is agreeing with us. There must be a way to speed things up; there must be a way to confirm with our own eyes that the good we do comes back to us.

And here is what it is.

22

The Simple Act of Understanding

Jesus said,

> *Ye shall know the truth,*
> *And the truth shall make you free.*

A seed planted in rocky soil grows very slowly or not at all. A seed planted in fertile soil grows quickly, even as we watch.

Our intentions and our understanding are everything if we hope to use the deep memory to produce a perfect life.

We cannot give our leftovers to others once in a while, with some vague hope of reward. We cannot give to others only because someone told us to. There is no power in giving without iron will and knowledge.

We must commit to giving. We must see clearly that no penny has ever come to us, except by giving. Deep in our hearts we must want to see this work for everyone in the world.

The simple act of knowing what we are doing, and why, makes it happen before our eyes.

23

Tracking Our Progress

Jesus said,

> *Wherever two or three are gathered*
> *together in my name,*
> *there am I in the midst of them.*

If seeing all these things work immediately in our own life requires iron will and knowledge, how are we to acquire these two qualities? By planting them, of course.

Here are four easy steps we take:

1. We track our progress by keeping a small spiritual diary. If what we seek is financial security, then before going to bed we write down three small things we have done today to provide others with this same security.
2. We let a friend know about our new program to provide for others. Every two weeks we invite our friend out for coffee and share some progress notes from our diary to see if our friend has any insights to share.

3. Once a day, we pick up the book you are holding now. We reread one or two of the sections, concentrating on the words of Christ.
4. We make a weekly habit of attending the church of our choice. Now no church or congregation is perfect until our own seeds are so. But we will certainly find the presence of Jesus and hear inspiring words to carry us on.

24

The Mustard Seed

Jesus said,

> *What thing compares most to the Kingdom of God? A mustard seed. Why? Because when you plant it, it is the smallest seed in the world; but then it grows, and becomes the largest of the plants in our garden, and birds come to rest in its shade.*

Another question should have come by now.

If the only way to reach a certain level of income is basically giving away the same amount, then what's the point? How do I actually get ahead of the game?

Have you ever seen an oak tree fall on a house or a car? Three tons of hardwood, all of it produced by a single acorn.

Seeds in the deep memory multiply in just the same way. Persons who provide a single day's needs for someone else can expect years of security in return.

But only if they have that iron determination and a matching *understanding* of the seeds.

25

A Very Christian Thing to Do

In making his sacrifice, Christ attains heaven, for us.

The most important question of all should have come to you by now: "It begins to sound as though the only reason to help others is to get something for ourselves. And that doesn't seem like a very Christian thing to do."

Think carefully. Suppose I get up from my chair at work and go to make a cup of coffee for someone else, knowing full well that I've just guaranteed myself quite a few cups of coffee when the seeds sprout later from my deep memory.

I've just doubled the number of people in the office who are getting a cup of coffee.

And that's a *very* Christian thing to do.

26

The End of Poverty

Jesus said,

> *Sell all that thou hast,*
> *and distribute unto the poor,*
> *and thou shalt have treasure.*

Where does money itself come from? Why is it that in our lifetime, after tens of thousands of years, it has suddenly become possible for almost everyone on the planet to write or speak to each other instantly, for only pennies? Where do these things come from?

The Bible says that God made the world; but it's clear that God made it so that we can receive only what we give to others.

And so if all of us give whatever we can to each other, then each one of us is comforted, and each one becomes wealthy.

It's not true that there's only so much wealth to go around in the world.

We will make new wealth, prosperity that covers all the world, in a way never seen before.

27

The End of Competition

Jesus said,

> *If any man sues thee in the court,*
> *and takes away your coat,*
> *then let him have thy cloak as well.*

Growing up, we were taught that we have to fight for what we want. We need to be stronger, smarter, and faster to get things before others get them first.

But now this idea of the deeper memory throws doubt on all we know. If it's true that we get only something that we've already given away to others, then we should be competing to *give* to others, not *take* from them.

The courage to do this needs a lot of this new knowledge.

There will come a day when, at work, we'll be smart enough to fight to get that promotion for *someone else*. And if the oil supply grows short in the world, we'll make sure our international competitors get theirs first.

28

The Delightful Confusion between "Me" and "You"

Jesus said,

Thou shalt love thy neighbor as thyself.

Everything we've said so far means that I can't get to what I want unless I go through you first. Without other people, nothing is possible for ourselves. I *need* you.

And so your interests become my interests.

Now this gets a little confusing, in a wonderful way, because the difference between my interests and your interests is — well — exactly what makes the difference between "me" and "you" in the first place.

And so we're also looking at the end of the very idea of "me" and "you."

29

How to Get That Dream House

Now the slave trader Habban sailed with Thomas south around Arabia and landed on the Malabar Coast of India. In fact, there are still today tens of thousands of Indians living there who are Christians and who claim to be spiritual descendants of St. Thomas.

The pair then worked up the coast and north along the Indus River to Taxila, a city the Tibetans call Dojok.

Here waited the king who had ordered an architect slave. He was known to the Greeks as Gondophores, and tradition says he was the king that the Romans called Gaspar. Gaspar was one of the three wise men from the East who had followed the star to Bethlehem, thirty years before, to greet the birth of Christ.

The king was delighted with the latest new slave. He went over the plans for his proposed palace with Thomas, made sure the disciple had all the funds he needed to get started, and promptly went on vacation.

Gaspar received regular and glowing reports from St. Thomas on the progress of the palace along with requests for more construction money, which the king happily sent.

The big day came, then, when Gaspar returned. He went to see his new palace, but not a single stone of it had been laid. Thomas had taken every penny of the money and given it away to poor people all around the kingdom.

Within the day, Thomas and Habban were languishing in chains in the dungeon below the old palace, while the king decided whether to strip off their skin or boil them alive in oil. The king's brother, by the name of Gad, was so upset by the theft that he had a heart attack and died.

That night, Gad was taken by the angels to heaven and shown a number of houses there to choose from. But one particularly fine palace caught his eye immediately. He asked if he could have it.

"Oh, no," replied the angels. "This one is reserved. It is the new palace of your brother, King Gaspar, which Thomas has built in heaven by giving away all the money to the poor."

Gad was no fool. He talked the angels into sending him back to earth so he could warn his brother that Thomas really had built the palace after all. And by the way he made a deal with Gaspar to buy his beautiful palace.

The moral of the story is this: do we have the courage and intelligence to build our dream house by giving away all our money for a house to those in the world who have no homes? Another inevitable step in removing the poverty of the world, and thus gaining for ourselves all that we ever dreamed of.

30

Heaven and Earth

Another question should be coming up by now. Didn't Jesus himself say,

> *Lay not up for yourselves treasures upon earth,*
> *where moth and rust corrupt,*
> *and thieves break through and steal.*
>
> *Lay up instead for yourselves*
> *treasures in heaven.*

Jesus seems clear that we should never hope for gain in this world. The palace that Thomas built for King Gaspar is over on the other side, in heaven.

We must absolutely understand what heaven and earth really mean. On this, the eastern teachings of Christ are a wonderful revelation.

Here is heaven: if we want a beautiful home we take what money we have and provide for those who have no homes.

We are determined, and we really understand what we're doing, and so the seeds ripen fast in the deeper memory. Our dream house emerges and it comes now, in this life, quickly.

And we naturally use our new house as a place from which to do all sorts of good things for others. These seeds ripen in turn, and things get better and better. Heavenly reinvestment—a continuous upward spiral.

At some point as the cycle takes us up, we cross over the line into heaven, and this happens "*before* we taste of death," as Jesus has said already.

If this is heaven, then where is the world? The world of pain, the world where moth and rust corrupt, is the world where we do not understand, and so we do not give first to others.

A dead-end world, a world where we take our money and spend it only on ourselves. To buy ourselves a house, where we live and grow old and die.

And don't think the children won't sell it.

31

Me Ye Have Not Always

A few last tips about prosperity and success. Do you know just when it was that Judas decided to betray Jesus? It was when a woman came and massaged an expensive oil into Christ's hair.

Judas and some others felt that the oil could have been sold and the money offered to the poor. But Jesus berates his disciples, saying that the woman will be praised for her deed by generations to come.

What we give comes back much more powerfully, depending on whom we give it to.

In order of increasing power, the very poor, or sick; those who have helped us in the past, especially our parents; and finally teachers and churches, without whom we would never understand to give.

32

The Rule of Ten Percent

Jesus said,

> *He that receiveth a prophet*
> *in the name of a prophet*
> *shall receive a prophet's reward.*

The eastern branch of Christianity teaches a wonderful method for piling up good seeds in the deeper memory. And it works for everything: for health, success, relationships, and everything else we could ever want.

People around us may not always be aware of how seeds in the deeper memory are forming their world, but nonetheless they do great good, all day long.

We also see countless people enjoying the rewards of good they have already done, again, whether or not they realize how it all works.

The simple art of feeling *happy* that others are doing good things, creating and receiving their rewards, is a reaffirmation of the truth that runs the universe.

As such, it's a potent seed that brings us, it is said, a full 10 percent of all the power of the goodness of others that we're celebrating. All without getting off the couch!

33

A Practical Note

Jesus said repeatedly that we should sell everything we own and give all the money away to the poor.

Admittedly we'd get some very powerful seeds if we did so. But would we be able to maintain our belief in these seeds, in the time it takes for them to come back to us? Doubts would begin to creep in.

Doubt is the great slayer of good seeds. And so at first, says the eastern family of Christ, we should go slowly and carefully. When we see results start to come, then we'll trust the process more, and then we can begin to increase our investment in humanity.

And so a practical rule of thumb: begin now to set aside 10 percent of every paycheck you receive, in a separate bank account. You won't miss it.

Watch the world for six months to see where your money would do the most good. And then give, give.

THREE

LOVE

34

The End of Love as We Know It

And so everything that ever happens to us in our entire life comes directly from what we do to others. We've seen how this idea basically junks all our old notions about things like health, money, competition, and even the idea of "you" and "me."

Let's see what it does to the concept of love.

We left St. Thomas in a dungeon in Taxila, up in the northwestern part of ancient India. This area is particularly important because here lie the mountain passes of the Hindu Kush. If you want to visit (or conquer) India overland from the West, you have to come through these passes.

And so for thousands of years, ideas have entered India by way of the land of Taxila.

Now when Thomas got to India, there were of course already old and wonderful religions there. Hinduism dates back thousands of years before Moses, and Buddhism surged through the country five hundred years before the birth of Christ.

But in the historical moment of Thomas's arrival, a kind of stagnation had set in among these faiths. Buddhism in particular had seen the union of two great ideas rise and then begin to fall.

These two ideas are the seeds of the deeper memory and the kind of love these seeds demand.

Here are the old kinds of love: romantic love, love for our family, love for the country we live in. But what happens to all these kinds of love in a world that is actually forming around how well I take care of *everyone* else?

In the generations immediately following Thomas's arrival, an incredible revolution of ideas swept across India—all based on a completely new and higher notion of love. It is given the name of Mahayana: the Greater Way.

We have coins and statues and buildings that attest to the flood of ideas that arrived in India from Greece and Rome and Jerusalem. We have books like the *Questions of King Milinda,* an extraordinary exchange between an Indian sage and the Greek king Menander. We see stunning links between Sanskrit, the ancient language of India, and the Greek and Latin first used to record the words of Jesus.

But of infinitely more importance is this new idea of love that burst into India after the death of Christ. Perhaps it was just a coincidence; perhaps it was the result of efforts by Thomas and like-minded people. Perhaps great ideas rise in the world in different places at the same time, or perhaps there is a higher power that delivers these messages without regard to the borders we draw between nations.

Or perhaps what history *was* is coming *now* from us, like the beauty of a painting.

In any case, let us now partake of this new and higher love.

35

Our Right to Love

We may be healthy and physically comfortable, but no life is complete without love, without deeper relationships shared with friends, family, and a partner for life.

This last is a basic human urge, an urge to unite the most basic energies of life — male and female, not just in a physical way but in the divine as well.

We have no real record of any physical relationship between Christ and Mary Magdalene, but the importance of the deeper bond they shared is something people have felt throughout history.

It's no coincidence that only Mary had the courage to seek the body of Christ; it's no coincidence that it was she who recognized him first.

36

The Three Steps

From the Gospel of St. John:

> *Mary turned back, and saw Jesus standing,*
> *and knew not that it was Jesus.*
>
> *Jesus saith unto her, Mary.*
> *She turned herself,*
> *and saith unto him, Master.*

There are three steps involved in every relationship between a man and a woman. First we have to find the other person. Once that person is found, we want to keep that person. And yet keeping our partner has no meaning unless we are also happy together.

Let's start with the first. Except, as you've probably already guessed, this business of the seeds in our deeper memory throws doubt upon the entire idea of *finding* our perfect partner.

It doesn't work that way. It never did. And you probably sense that as well.

37

Planes That Fly, Sometimes

You know that old saying,

God helps those who help themselves.

There's something amazing about the way we go about our lives. We don't really know what we're doing.

Suppose you were about to fly on a new airline. The flight attendant stops you at the door of the plane and asks you to sign an insurance waiver before getting on board.

"Why?" you ask. "Is there something wrong?"

"Not at all," she smiles reassuringly. "It's just that, you know, we don't *quite* have this flying thing figured out completely. But there's every chance we won't crash at all!"

You'd turn around fast and go find a real airline, right?

If you think about it, though, we do things all the time without really knowing whether or not they're going to work out for us. We live all day by guesswork.

Well, let's take the guesswork out of finding a partner.

38

The Two Bad Choices Trick

Then Pilate said unto Jesus,

Do you not hear all the witnesses here who accuse you?

And Jesus answered him not a word, and at this Pilate marveled greatly.

Times come to us when we need to make a decision between two options: should I say this or should I say that?

Two choices. Always two choices, and always both of them wrong.

There's an old sales scam called the "two bad choices trick." We walk in to buy a car, and the salesman takes us over to two models.

"This one has a great color," he begins, "but the engine's not so good." We frown. He immediately points to the other.

"This one works great, with a hundred bucks off for all the dents. So which one do you want?"

Our mind suddenly freezes, forced between two bad choices. He nails it down with, "And how will you pay for that?"

39

Option Three

Jesus said,

Get thee behind me, Satan.

Now a used car dealer may or may not be the devil. But if Satan does exist — and he does — then he enjoys nothing more than to see us waste our lives away struggling between two bad choices.

For example:

1. If I want to trim down a bit,
   Should I jog or do yoga instead?
2. If I'm putting aside a nest-egg for retirement,
   Should I go for a risky investment, or a conservative one?
3. Am I more likely to meet someone nice at church?
   Or should I try on-line?

We know the answer by now: none of the above. Because none of these choices works *all the time.*

It's not *how* we meet our partner; it's *why.* Why? Because the seeds were there, and nothing else.

The Tibetans call this Option Three. Plant the seeds: it's the only choice that actually works.

40

First Paint a Picture

Gideon said,

> *I have seen an angel of the Lord, face to face.*

First sit down and decide exactly what you want in a partner. With the deeper memory, nothing is impossible — so don't be shy. Good-looking, intelligent, and sensitive too.

Don't settle for less than what you really want. We're not stuck between two old cars anymore.

If you already have a partner, then make the list anyway. There's nothing about anyone around us that we can't change — by working on ourselves first.

A good trick to get this change to come faster is a special kind of prayer. It's called pattern prayer.

41

Masters of the Art of Prayer

Perhaps the most noticeable contribution that came out of the wave that swept across India in the centuries after Thomas was a high refinement of the art of prayer, or meditation, which continues to this day. We can learn a lot from this.

The Indians sometimes say that if Taxila in northwest India was the head — the doorway for wisdom from the West — then Bengal in the northeast was the heart.

For a thousand years, wise men and women shuttled back and forth across the top of India, in the shadow of the Himalayas, carrying ideas. A famous spiritual center grew at Taxila, and a sister school blossomed two thousand miles to the east, at Nalanda.

Both were wiped out by invasions of India a thousand years after Christ.

Luckily for us, the knowledge possessed at these centers was transplanted to Tibet, just in the nick of time. Masters like the one named Kamala Shila literally walked over the mountain chains of Mount Everest, carrying into Tibet priceless spiritual jewels, including the new conception of love that had arrived with Thomas.

Now Kamala Shila (whose name means "The Fragrance of a Good Person") was actually called to Tibet by its king around 750 A.D. There was an argument going on about how to pray.

In ancient India and Tibet, disagreements of a religious nature were settled in an intriguing way. One person was chosen by the king to represent each side of the question. In this case, a Chinese monk called Hwashang came to argue that the best kind of prayer or meditation is simply sitting with an empty head, not thinking about anything.

Kamala Shila, on the other hand, walked all the way to Tibet from Nalanda in India just to argue the opposite idea: when we pray, we must focus the mind on the most important and beautiful thing we can imagine. And that is love — the love where we work for others through the magic of the deeper memory.

As ancient tradition demanded, both sides appeared on the appointed day at the court of the king, in a place called Samye. Citizens from across the country came to attend the debate, and when it was all over they helped decide which side had proved its point successfully.

This system had been in use for over two thousand years, and the stakes were high. The side that lost — meaning everyone in the whole country who followed the ideas of the debater who failed — was required to join the faith of the side that won.

Thus it was that a rich and mighty tradition of prayer took root among the descendants of the ideas that Thomas helped bring to India. One final argument convinced the king and everyone present that prayer takes a lot more skill than just emptying out your mind.

If you pray about nothing, said Kamala Shila, then you get nothing. The harder you try *not* to think, well then the harder you're thinking!

So let us think in our prayer upon love — the highest form of love. We can start quite happily with a higher love for the partner we're looking for. Let us have the courage to have our cake and eat it too.

Here then is how to *pray* a partner into being.

42

Pattern Prayer

Jesus said,

> *Do not think that prayer consists*
> *of the useless repetition of words.*

Let's get one thing straight right away. There's a certain kind of prayer that doesn't work. We figured that out in third grade when we prayed for a new red bike for Christmas, and nothing happened.

The eastern tradition of Christ offers us an entire toolbox filled with different methods of prayer. Each one is used for a different purpose. There's pattern prayer, calming prayer, focus prayer, problem-solving prayer, awareness prayer, heart prayer, requesting prayer, and thanksgiving prayer.

Pattern prayer means we very purposely review a certain picture or idea inside our mind, over and over, every day.

This pattern then gets burned into the mind. It sinks into the deeper memory and affects the seeds that lie there.

Keep picturing exactly how you want your partner to be. With the right good deeds to back it up, the person you seek will emerge. You didn't *find* that person; you *made* them.

43

The Proof Is That We're Here

Jesus said,

They have their reward.

Another question should be popping up in your mind by now. Suppose I'm attracted to a certain person at work, but that person hardly ever notices me? I understand how if I want to see more beauty around me, then I have to plant the seeds for that in myself by providing beauty for others. But how am I going to get that person to see *me* as beautiful?

There's a really important point here. It's definitely *not* the case that we can do the work for others and plant seeds inside of them. If I could somehow be doubly good for a week and then dump these seeds into your soul, then none of us would be here now, in a world of war and pain and children who die in accidents.

Certainly there are enough good people who have come before us. Certainly they would have given us all their seeds by now, without us even asking.

44

Thy Faith Hath Made Thee Whole

But wasn't it the whole point of the crucifixion that Christ gave up his life for our sins? In a way, hasn't he already given us his good seeds, or at least taken away our bad seeds?

A woman was healed by Jesus, who then said to her, "Thy faith hath made thee whole."

We'll talk more about this point later, but it's important to start on it now. We've been saying all along that good things happen to us when we do them first for others. It *is* possible for a person like Jesus to heal us, but not by moving his seeds into our deep memory: not by being good *for* us. This we must obviously do ourselves, or else God and Moses and Jesus wouldn't constantly harp on us to keep their holy commandments.

One of the greatest seeds we can ever plant, though, is simply to adore and believe in the One who has brought us this knowledge of seeds.

This one seed of faith is so powerful that — as we'll see — miracles can happen: miracles that, in the end, have come from ourselves.

45

The Eye of the Beholder

Pilate asked Jesus,

Are you the King of the Jews?

And Jesus answered him,

Thou sayest it.

Back to how we get someone to see us as attractive. It's absolutely true that how someone else sees *us* depends on *their* seeds. But how *we* see *them* see *us* is coming from *our* seeds!

In Christ's eastern teachings this kind of seed is called an "environmental seed." If we're constantly careful to honor and protect life in the world, then of course we ourselves get healthier and stronger.

But these seeds also produce a bigger result. We begin to see more health in the entire world around us: people live longer; medical science makes breakthroughs.

Realize, though, one thing. The very people that we see as more healthy may or may not see *themselves* that way. They may even feel worse than before. Where lies the beauty in a painting?

Love, and you will see love. You will *be* loved.

46

The Correlations

Let's summarize then how we find/make our ideal partner. Jesus asked,

Do men gather grapes of thorns?

Which means, there must absolutely be a *consistency* between what we do and what we get. If you want grapes, you don't plant a cactus.

So first we practice that clear, constant, mental picture of the husband, wife, or companion we want. We were talking about someone who was attractive, intelligent, and sensitive. So what are the corresponding seeds for these three qualities?

The seed for seeing people as attractive is, again, strictly avoiding anger. Since the beauty is coming from us, even someone we've lived with for years will change, physically, before our very eyes.

The best seed to plant for being around intelligent people is simply to review, constantly, the ultimate intelligence of seeing where things really come from.

And sensitivity to everyone around us creates it in our partner. Almost every other quality works the same way: use common sense; be what you seek.

47

Whatever It Takes

Peter got down out of the boat and began to walk across the water to Jesus. But then he doubted and began to sink.

There's one really important thing we'd better cover about *finding* our partner, before we go on to *keeping* that partner.

By now you've probably had the thought, "But I'm not really a person who gets angry so much — surely not as often as some people I know! So why hasn't this gorgeous person already shown up in my life?"

The answer is the question. It's simply not enough. It's not enough that we don't blow up that often. If you really want gorgeous, then we're talking about not getting the slightest bit annoyed, even when somebody hits you with something really serious.

Work harder. You'll know it when you're there: the day that gorgeous appears.

48

Roadblocks

One more thing we'd better cover, or else we may be waiting much longer for gorgeous than we need to.

A particularly persistent family carried a paralyzed man on a stretcher to the house where Jesus was staying. The house was already packed with people, so they broke through the thatch of the roof and lowered the man down to Christ. Jesus helps the crippled man remove his sins, and this in itself is enough for him to get up and walk away.

We planted a lot of negative seeds before we ever heard about seeds. And they're still there, creating roadblocks.

We may be patient people now, but if we've been angry in the past, then gorgeous won't arrive until those seeds are finished.

Let's see how to remove these old bad seeds. That in itself might be enough for us to get up and walk.

49

Gorgeous Confessions

Jesus healed another cripple, saying—

Behold, thou art made whole: go and sin no more.

Suppose we've made a serious effort to plant the right seeds for an attractive partner: we've made ourselves into a person who is nearly incapable of anger. But sometimes we still might not see results. This is a sign that we have a roadblock from old seeds of anger, whether we remember these past incidents or not.

We take two steps to remove these old seeds:

1. Find someone you respect—a member of the clergy or a sincere friend—and admit to that person openly any anger you've had in the past.
2. Resolve to remove any anger that is left over now and dedicate this power to destroying the old seeds. The better you keep this resolution, the faster the roadblocks will disappear.

This cleansing confession is not a ritual or guilt trip. It's just a very smart way to speed up gorgeous. Use it as well for any old bad seeds that are blocking your health and prosperity.

50

Never-Ending Beauty

Now gorgeous will arrive. But how to keep gorgeous?

Jesus warned us against things of the world, where "moth and rust corrupt." One of the saddest events of life is when love comes and then leaves, or even turns to contempt.

Now that we know about seeds, it's easy to see why things fall apart. A relationship grows like a tree, from a seed. As the seed turns into the tree, it spends its power and disappears. Left to itself, the tree too will grow and die, as the power imparted by the seed wears out.

This is the way of all things in the world of suffering. And it doesn't have to happen.

Heaven is different. In a divine world *we keep planting seeds*, and relationships don't fall apart. They just keep getting better and better.

In our example, be strictly patient with gorgeous, beginning on your first day together and continuing forever after. Beauty will continue always to flower, higher and higher.

51

More Stupid Than Immoral

Jesus said,

Thou shalt not commit adultery.

One of the great tragedies of modern life is the romantic mystique that has built up around the crass act of breaking up other people's relationships and marriages — causing immeasurable pain to partners and their children — all for some brief service of our sexual organ.

It's not just that stealing someone else's partner is wrong or immoral. Rather, it's just plain stupid. We are denying ourselves the very thing we want.

If we succeed in taking away someone else's partner, *it's because we've respected other people's relationships in the past.* By breaking up a relationship now, *we guarantee ourselves miserable relationships for years to come.*

Don't be confused by the time it takes for seeds to grow.

52

Sharing

Finding and keeping a partner is one thing. But we see a lot of marriages where people simply suffer together quietly for years.

It's not enough to *be* with each other; we want to be *happy* with each other. Here then are a few tips from the eastern family. There are a lot more coming up in the next section called "Happiness."

Jesus said,

> *A man and a wife*
> *are no longer two people,*
> *but one flesh.*

In any relationship, one partner may come to dominate in some way: one decides how money is spent or what the couple does when they're together. We have to catch ourselves if we begin taking over the relationship in this way.

Voluntarily and completely sharing this kind of authority between us is a key to harmony — whether at work or at home. The more quietly and joyfully we can surrender decisions and possessions to our partner, the looser the borders between us become, until finally we overlap completely.

53

Infinite Borders

Someone came and told Jesus that his family was waiting outside to see him. Christ stretched forth his hand toward the crowd of disciples around him and said, "Behold my family!"

Let us not make our relationship an excuse to transfer our old selfishness to the two of us, or to ourselves and our children. We cannot be happy in a family that ignores the needs of the larger world, any more than we can be happy as individuals who ignore the needs of other individuals.

When we both care as much for the pain of a stranger as we do for the pain of our partner, when we care as much for the pain of children halfway around the world as we do for the pain of the children within the confines of our little house, then the happiness within our family is equally boundless.

54

A Peek Ahead

Just after the crucifixion, Christ appeared and walked down a country road with two of his disciples, discussing how the apparent disaster might have had a higher purpose. The disciples don't recognize Jesus for hours, until they stop together at an inn for dinner; Jesus blesses and breaks the bread, and then —

Their eyes were opened and they knew him.

A final note about enjoying this relationship with our partner. Divine beings have infinite power and love us infinitely. They also have infinite patience; and so ten or twenty years is as nothing to them.

Which is to say, there's absolutely no reason why a holy being who wanted to stay close to us and guide us couldn't show up as our partner and spend a lifetime this way, anonymously, helping us steer our way.

Think of that next time you feel like there's not enough glamour in your life.

55

Love and the Deeper Memory

We've covered now the basic foundation of a happy life: good health, physical security, and a successful relationship. With these in hand, we can turn to the higher goals of a human existence.

Remember, though, what we've been saying all along. We need the courage to get *everything* out of life: the courage to go for it all. We're not trading happiness in this life for happiness in some life beyond. We're *using* happiness of this life *as a path* to higher happiness, as the beginning of a higher existence. Let's have our cake and eat it too.

Again, it's crucial to see what makes this all possible: the new kind of love that swept, like a wave, from the Cross and on to India and Tibet, through Thomas.

In the beginning we love people just because they're people. Next we love people because we see how life is doomed to death and pain. And then finally we graduate to a love of real hope: a love that knows that the problems of the world come from the seeds in our own deep memory.

A higher love, because now we have the knowledge we need to stop all the pain of the ones we love, forever.

FOUR

HAPPINESS

56

What Is Happiness?

Jesus said,

> *These things I have spoken unto you*
> *that in me you might have peace.*

It's important to realize that there are certain types of seeds for strength, security, and love — but a completely *different* set of seeds for *happiness*. There are lots of famous, beautiful, and successful people who are absolutely miserable.

The eastern branch of the Christian family describes true happiness as the final victory over our own mental demons — all the negative emotions that cloud the human heart.

These negative thoughts are said to come in thousands of variations; let's go through some of the main ones now and see how we wage our war against them. For it truly is a war, a war within our own minds, and we must train and equip ourselves as spiritual soldiers in the battle for happiness.

57

Demons Are for Slaying

Jesus confronted the demons and forced them to enter the bodies of a herd of swine; the swine ran violently down a steep place into the sea and perished in the waters.

Let's get one thing straight about this war we're about to declare. We're not talking about how to *cope* with the painful regions of our heart; we're not talking about finding comfort in our suffering, or even about finding a way to grow in the midst of challenges.

We're talking about peace itself: about destroying negative emotions within us, not for a few days or hours, but forever. Nothing left to *cope* with.

And we can do it, for one single reason. Think about it. If the way we see a painting or our partner is coming from us — from how we've treated others — then *so is the way we experience our own thoughts*. It is *we* who make our own minds a heaven or hell to live in.

This knowledge is our invincible weapon. Here's how to use it.

58

We Know Not

Then said Jesus,

Father, forgive them,
for they know not
what they do.

All the mental demons that spoil our happiness boil down to misunderstanding how the seeds in the deep memory work. Understand this misunderstanding and we can reach perfect happiness.

Only when we actively misunderstand the world, only in ignorance, can a mental demon arise. And the demons themselves always belong to one of two families: *liking* something ignorantly or *disliking* something ignorantly.

59

Anger

Jesus said,

> *Why is it that you notice a piece of sawdust in your brother's eye, but not the plank of wood in your own?*

Since we've been on the subject of anger, let's tackle this demon first. How are we disliking something in an ignorant way here?

Someone calls us stupid. That's unpleasant, and it's totally right to dislike it. But dislike it in a *smart* way. A way that prevents it from happening again.

When someone speaks harshly to us, it's a picture emerging from our own deep memory — a picture that was planted when we said an unkind thing to someone else earlier on.

This simple insight means the end of anger, forever. The other person is only an agent who delivers to us what we ourselves have mailed. The single most stupid thing we could do now would be to respond to the person angrily, planting the seed for the next unpleasant person we meet.

60

Irritation

Jesus said,

> *He that is faithful in that which is least*
> *is faithful also in much.*

Cigarettes are little things, but enough of them can kill us as dead as being hit by a truck.

A few minutes of violent anger at a person or an object have the unique ability to enter the deep memory and destroy large pockets of good seeds: weeks or months of good deeds done toward others.

Irritation does the same, quietly and steadily. Complaining about the weather or work; constant, low-level bickering with family members; moaning about the world in general actually *make* our world worse. And then we complain *more* and . . . you get the point.

There's a great weapon to fight that disturbing tendency toward constant irritation or grumpiness that we discover growing within ourselves as the years pass. It's called "awareness prayer."

We stop at regular points during the day — let's say in that private moment when we offer our food, just before we eat anything — and check in with our state of mind. Has that unfocused grouchiness slipped in during the last few hours? Ask it to leave, not because the world isn't a hard place sometimes, but because there's no sense in making it worse.

And then suddenly things get brighter.

61

Envy

Jesus takes up the cup at the last supper of his life — and what are the disciples talking about?

> *There began an argument between them, as to which of them would be considered greatest of the disciples.*

Jealousy is another low-level poison that slowly drains away our happiness. It is best combated, as usual, with the raw power of understanding.

I can have only those things that I first provide to others. And so I succeed only when others succeed before me. To be unhappy that others have found anything at all that makes them happy is not only unpleasant and ignoble, but also seriously stupid.

Strange to live in a culture where passing gas in company is considered bad manners, but not standing with others and wishing that they weren't so happy.

62

Sadness

We wonder how Christ healed even lepers or the blind. But we miss the more amazing thing. He *wanted* to heal them. *He stopped and noticed that they needed healing.*

Sadness is a general bickering at the world that has seeped down inside of us. Its single distinguishing feature is that we're now completely focused on *how bad I feel.* Other people and their problems are forgotten entirely.

The cure is painfully obvious. We live in a world where we can escape pain only if we help others escape it first. We must struggle — and it *is* a struggle — to use this weapon of knowledge, to make *some* attempt to reach out of our sadness and help someone else out of sadness too.

Knowledge of the seeds is like sunlight, good earth, clean water. Even a tiny act of concern for others — if done within knowledge — is enough of a seed to dispel our sadness.

63

Depression

Jesus said,

> *To this end was I born,*
> *to bear witness unto the truth.*

Pilate replied,

> *What is truth?*

A darkness suddenly descends, often without warning or apparent cause. And now everything is darkness. Our work, our friends, our world.

And then it lifts, and something makes us laugh, and we wonder how we could have been so wrong about things. Such is depression.

What is reality? What is true? The descent of darkness or our life before or after it? You can call depression abnormal, but the darkness it sees is real, for it too comes from seeds of how we've treated others.

The cure is radical and effective. In the depths of the darkness, we *use* the darkness. We gather it all at our heart and then go forth and gather more from others who are depressed, until our heart is full of darkness. And then in the selfsame moment we see a burst of golden light within our heart, and the darkness is burnt to cinder.

This is the first half of what the eastern family calls "heart prayer." By taking on the pain of others in our own darkest moments, upon our own small cross, we destroy all pain.

64

Insomnia

Jesus said,

You are the light of the world.

A great many of our mental demons feed on a simple lack of sleep. And then we have more trouble sleeping, and new demons come.

The second half of the practice of heart prayer is a wonderful cure for insomnia. Lie down to sleep and close your eyes. Take ten slow breaths, concentrating only on the breath, just counting to ten.

Then begin to imagine a few of the people in nearby homes, also going to bed. Certainly some of them have trouble sleeping too.

Imagine a ball of toasty warm, golden light within your heart. It is calmness, peace. Now send the ball slowly through the air, through the walls, to settle in the heart of one person nearby who cannot fall asleep. See your neighbor sleep then, with the warmth you've provided.

Continue until you wake up, bright and refreshed.

65

Lack of Energy

When Jesus finally reveals the true extent of his power by raising Lazarus from the dead, a very strange thing happens. Leaders who will one day have to die themselves, leaders with their own loved ones who will die as well, feel threatened. They begin to plot the murder of Christ.

Nobody asks him how he did it. Nobody really *thanks* Jesus much in any of the Gospels.

Being thankful is the key to cure a lack of energy — and all varieties of laziness and procrastination.

The eastern family of Christ prescribes thankfulness prayer when we feel heavy or tired. Fix yourself a nice cup of coffee or cocoa, flop down on the couch, and just purposely send your mind off on the tour of your life, past and present.

Think of every single person who's ever helped you, and thank them mentally. For goodness sake, even the clerks at the grocery store are giving up the precious hours of their life for us. So get up, get going, and make something of yourself, to pay them all back!

66

Low Self-Esteem

Jesus said,

> *I tell you truly, that many prophets and righteous men have desired to see those things which ye see, and have not seen them.*

Meditating upon how much we already have, spending time in prayer every day to recall all there is for us to give thanks for, also cures any lack of self-esteem or confidence that we might be feeling.

Realize one thing. The act of drawing a single breath in this life requires countless seeds planted by serving others. And we have so much more: we have freedom; we live in prosperity; we can *think*.

Our very lives are proof of just how good we are inside. To hear the name of Jesus once in an entire lifetime requires immense pools of kindness in our deeper memory.

We ourselves are on the verge of angelhood, as soon you will see. Remember who you are.

67

Funlessness

Only Jesus would pause on the way to a violent death and joke:

> *It's easier to squish a camel through the eye of a needle than to get a rich man into heaven.*

By the way, he's talking about dead-end rich, of course. Where we stop reinvesting our money in others.

Creativity, spontaneity, and plain old good humor sometimes seem to desert us for weeks. There's an easy way to get them back.

As we walk through a single day in our lives, at work and at home, we see others creating: songs, books, buildings, products. Stop for a moment to appreciate them.

Who would have thought of that? What a pleasure to see people who are so *good* at what they do!

Within a few days, you'll be fun again. Keep it up!

68

Anxiety

The disciples saw Jesus walking on the sea and cried out for fear, thinking it was an evil spirit.

Jesus spoke to them, saying —

> *Be of good cheer, it is I;*
> *Be not afraid.*

They're having layoffs at work, and I'm swimming in anxiety. Let's check in with our understanding of what we should do. Start reading the want ads, just in case? Or work those extra hours that our supervisor asks for, just to stay on her good side?

You're right — that's just the old two bad choices trick. Because neither approach works. Because neither approach *always* works. Admit it.

The only thing that will surely help save our job is to make sure that we do our best to help *other* people at work keep *their* jobs.

Learn to be smart, smart fearless. It sounds crazy. But then so does most of what Jesus tells us to do. Because we're so used to falling for the two bad choices.

69

Nervousness

After Lazarus, Jesus turns his steps toward Jerusalem, where he says he will die.

The disciples were amazed
that he went—
and as they followed,
they were afraid.

Our own nerves are less glorious but just as real. Look around the bus on the ride to work. Fidgeting, tapping fingers, jerking feet, frowns washing across the faces. Life makes us nervous.

Here's a good example of coping, and then curing.

We can cope with nervousness by using focus prayer. Call up a little picture of Christ in your mind, gentle and reassuring. Move it down from your head to your heart, and then to your lower back, just below the waist. Let him stay here, warm and grounding, throughout the day. Your nervousness will lessen.

The cure, though, must come through others. Keep an eye out for nervous people around you. That waitress looks new: give her an encouraging word. The seeds for your own nerves melt away.

70

Attention Disorders

Throughout the New Testament, Christ is constantly going away by himself for some silent focus — whether to a mountain or a quiet garden.

The eastern family says that we need time to focus as much as we need food itself.

We try to relax in the modern world, but relaxation doesn't seem to relax us: we sit and punch through TV channels aimlessly, we surf restlessly through the Web, and suddenly two hours are gone and we don't know where. Our children can't seem to focus through a brief conversation.

Attention disorders have a brief and simple cure. We respect others' need for some uninterrupted quiet. Let the cashier concentrate on finishing the last sale before you speak to him. Stop overloading friends with useless information. Sit with someone in silence, once a week.

Peaceful focus will return.

71

Living in the Past, or Future

Christ had this talent for turning disasters into triumphs. The leader of a tiny cult is stripped, flayed, and nailed up to die; and for the next two thousand years a large part of humanity considers it the greatest accomplishment in history.

There's a special mental demon that keeps us stuck in the past— in the good old days. Back when my life and the world at large were going right. Or else we're always off at this afternoon's appointment instead of enjoying the guest who's across the table from us now, this morning.

We can fight this demon or just get on his back and ride him to our goal.

Sure your boyfriend back in high school was cute. Go ahead, enjoy the memory. But as you do, reflect on how he didn't just happen by accident. You had seeds in you that made him come. Seeds planted by refusing the act of anger.

Come up out of the memory fresh and inspired. Go ahead and plan for the future: staying calm so gorgeous will reappear.

72

Grief

Jesus said,

Let the dead bury their dead.

We lose someone close to us. Here's how to cope with grief and then cure it.

The eastern family says that our minds are particularly vulnerable as we grieve. This is not a time for rash action or dwelling on things morosely. Be with friends, take walks, put yourself under the sun and blue sky.

But this is also a time of truth. Life is treacherous and, without knowledge like that which Christ has granted us, a frankly futile enterprise.

The death of a loved one can give us a new sense of purpose, a sense of urgency. Jesus claimed that death could be overcome, literally.

Don't let them have died in vain. Don't become one of the living dead. You owe it to them to see if death can be changed. Finish this book.

73

Obsession: Food, Sex, Possessions

A man asked Christ how he could win eternal life. Jesus advised him to get rid of all his possessions.

The man walked away, shaking his head. It's the last we hear of him.

We need food, and there's no reason that it shouldn't be food we find tasty. Intimacy and warmth are precious jewels sprinkled through our days here. And a sturdy, good-looking coat becomes a friend as it protects us over the years.

But there's this other way of relating to food and sex and possessions. A kind of restlessness, where we swallow a bag of chips without even *enjoying* the experience.

Take time and cook a delicious, healthy meal for someone else. Take a sincere, warm interest in someone else's life: ask someone about her work and *listen.* Think hard and make a modest, heartfelt gift of clothing to someone else.

Obsession returns to honest pleasure.

74

Addiction

Jesus said,

Thou shalt love thy neighbor as thyself.

Alcohol, drugs, and other forms of addiction have been around for as long as people have. We've struggled for thousands of years to find ways of curing them.

In light of the deeper memory, it's no surprise that the most consistently successful approach is for one person with an addiction problem to mentor and support another. Only by loving someone else as we do ourselves, only by giving someone what we ourselves seek, can we be free of this particular demon.

Make the process very conscious. At the core, and every day, must be a few minutes' review of this one truth: I will be healed only if I stop to help someone else be healed.

Then go out and enroll in some program where you help someone else with an addiction. Lord knows there are plenty of us.

75

Pride

Jesus said,

The last shall be first.

Pride is one of the mental demons that we are normally unaware of until it causes a disaster. It's also an interesting mix of *wanting* something in an ignorant way and *disliking* something, just as stupidly, at the same time.

We want to be famous, we want all the attention, we want to run the show. And if anyone else happens to gain some position or win some praise, we feel a sort of offended anger.

It's not wrong to want to be the best; then we can really help others. But play it smart on how to get there. It's difficult, but lots of fun once you get started.

Whenever there's a chance to get some attention, push someone else you know into the limelight and step back. Learn to let others do most of the talking, and listen honestly for things you can learn.

People will like you a lot more. And they'll also follow you, for these are the seeds.

76

Loss of Faith

Then entered Satan into Judas.

We see or hear something at church that shatters our faith. We even start to think about leaving. Here are some tips about coping and the cure for this disastrous mental demon.

If you think it over, giving up our own spiritual path because someone else has failed to follow it properly just doesn't make any sense. The path is not at fault; it's still a good road for getting us where we want to go. We don't give up driving cars because we hear that someone else has irresponsibly damaged theirs.

The cure here though is a difficult pill to swallow. Do we have sufficient intelligence and strength for it? All the qualities that we see in other people — and particularly the things that disturb us the most — are coming from our own deeper memory, from something we ourselves have done before. Other people's failings are a mirror of our own.

So let us root out all traces of this same weakness in ourselves. The way we experience church suddenly becomes pure sunlight.

77

Selfishness

Jesus said,

> *This is my commandment,*
> *That ye love one another,*
> *as I have loved you.*

Let's summarize this new path to happiness, taught by Jesus and illuminated by the eastern tradition of Thomas.

All the different mental demons that ruin our happiness are based on either liking or disliking something in an ignorant way. We want something, so we hurt others to get it. Or we want to avoid something, and we hurt others to get away from it.

Both actions, though, only bring us unhappiness, because they break the one rule that the universe works by: we can have only what we first provide to others, because everything is coming from our own deeper memory — from seeds we planted by taking care of others or by ignoring their needs.

The act of selfishness then becomes the single most stupid thing we can do, hurting ourselves as much as others.

Let us instead love one another, in the same shining knowledge with which Christ loves us.

FIVE

FREEDOM

78

Freedom from Useless

Ecclesiastes says,

> *I have seen every human activity that is done under the sun; and behold, all is useless, and simple frustration of the human spirit.*

We have a strong and healthy body; all our physical needs are covered. We find a relationship, and we are finally, really happy.

The number of marriages that end nowadays in bitter divorce is painful. But perhaps more painful is to see a couple work for years and finally become one — only to have death arrive and tear them from each other.

All that we ever do is useless. Whatever happiness we find must be lost. We cannot even keep our own flesh; we are stripped in the end even of our name.

Until we find freedom from death itself, nothing else has much meaning.

79

The Lie of the Metaphor

Jesus said,

> *I tell you the truth; the truth.*
> *If a person follows what I say,*
> *then they shall never see death.*

He said,

> *The righteous shall go into life eternal.*

Now one of the great achievements of the Devil in the time from the crucifixion up to now must surely be how these words have become only a metaphor.

Christ didn't mean it literally. Really good people get to live forever, but only after they suffer through death. Then they get to go to some vague place and somehow sit around with Jesus until the end of time.

But that's not at all what Jesus meant. He meant that we can stop death itself and give life its ultimate meaning. The teaching on how to do this is still held clear and strong among the eastern branch of our Christian family.

80

The Teaching Lives

Jesus said,

You shall pass from death unto life.

We now undertake one of the most important parts of this little book: the teaching on how not to die, the teaching on eternal life. This and the teaching that comes after it — the teaching on *what to do with* our eternal life — are alive and well in the mountains of snow.

The course of study in a Tibetan monastery is almost exactly the same now as it was a thousand years ago. Why change something that works? Five great subjects are studied. For a scriptural archeologist, they provide a delightful historical record of how the knowledge of life came to the east.

The first subject is called Discipline. This is a huge collection of guidelines from the earliest days of Buddhism, twenty-five hundred years old, on how to be a good person. The rules sound a lot like our own earliest teachings, the Old Testament: "Thou shalt not kill!" — which, as we've seen, is a crucial key to remaining strong and healthy.

But here, as in the Old Testament, you don't really feel as though *how it works* has been explained all that clearly. No great detail about the deeper memory: about *how* it is that the seeds come back to us.

The second subject studied is called the Art of Reasoning: how to think straight. This topic is vital, since so much about the spiritual world is beyond our physical senses. Exploring the realm of death is not like eating an apple: in the beginning, we must see our way with the eyes of deduction.

Here we feel distinctly the influence of the Greeks, as Alexander the Great broke through to western India in the land of Taxila, 320 years before Christ. When Alexander first embarked on his twelve-year journey of conquest, he even dragged along a fellow named Kallisthenes to keep a written account of his achievements for the folks back home. Kallisthenes was the nephew of Alexander's teacher, and this teacher was none other than Aristotle, the greatest logician in history.

Over the course of the next five centuries, as Greek kings flourished in India and were finally absorbed into the local population, an Aristotelian rigor and systematization entered Indian thinking. It came to stay in Tibet, where even today the distinctive hats worn during public philosophical debates are modeled after the plumed helmets of Greek and Roman soldiers.

The third monastic subject is called Higher Knowledge. It's based on a book called *The Treasure House,* written by an Indian wise man named Vasu Bandhu. The book is an important milestone in our spiritual timeline, for Master Vasu Bandhu composed it at the very moment of history when the new wave of a higher love flooded across India in the footsteps of St. Thomas and others.

Vasu Bandhu was in the middle of it, traveling frequently between the spiritual centers of Thomas's Taxila in the west and Nalanda in the east. He wrote *The Treasure House* as sort of an encyclopedia recording the state of spiritual knowledge in India prior to the arrival of the new wave; he saw the radical changes coming and in a way sealed the past. *The Treasure House* contains more information on the seeds of deeper memory, but it is still short on explaining the workings of this memory in detail.

The fourth subject is called the Perfection of Wisdom. The crucial part here for our spiritual history book is the teaching of a school of thought named the Mind Only. Of primary importance for this movement are the writings of Master Asangha, who was the brother of Vasu Bandhu.

Asangha is one of the first to embrace the new wave fully, reveling in its higher explanation of love. Without his clear descriptions of how the experiences of our life emerge from the deeper memory, we can hardly tackle the problem of death.

Master Asangha's explanation of these images closely resembles the thinking of Plato, Aristotle's own teacher. Early Christians considered these ideas very important and useful: in the library of Nag Hammadi, where we first found the *Gospel of St. Thomas,* the only pre-Christian material is a fragment of one of Plato's texts, the *Republic.* The few pages found here talk about the role that mental images play in how we see the world and how our own actions affect these images.

The ultimate weapon in our battle against death, though, is the fifth subject, called the Middle Way. By this time, about six centuries after Christ, the wisdom of East and West has been fully integrated: we come to a state of love that is fully aware that *what* we love is coming from *how* we love.

Here we learn to stay in the middle of the road and not to fall into the ditch on either side. With death, for example, we realize that it is not what it appears to be: it is not an unchangeable thing "out there." Even death is coming from how I have acted toward others in the past. We thus avoid falling off one side of the path.

And this fact itself keeps us out of the ditch on the opposite side: the very wrong idea that, if something is coming from my own deeper memory, then somehow it is less than real; for death is certainly something we very much need to deal with.

This last then was still the state of Christian wisdom within its eastern context a thousand years ago, when sages like Kamala Shila walked it over the Himalayas, from Nalanda into Tibet. And there it has been preserved, a cup for us to drink from now, the water of eternal life.

81

The Body Kills Itself

God said to Adam,

Dust thou art, and unto dust shalt thou return.

The eastern family says that we cannot defeat death unless we first truly believe that we *are* going to die. And none of us really believe we will die.

So every day we stop for a moment to do a brief prayer, the type the Tibetans call problem-solving prayer. This is used for convincing ourselves of something we're not so sure about, by going over the logic for it in our mind.

Will I die? Come on. Look at the world around you. The wealthy die, the powerful die, the young and healthy die, and they always have. What makes us think we're going to be any exception?

We could lock ourselves up in a sterilized bank vault. We could sit inside it and eat only organic foods and vitamins. We could even exercise regularly!

And still the body would kill us. If nothing outside of us kills us, our own body still kills us from the inside, a traitor to itself. We were born to die.

82

I Will Die Today

Isaac said,

I know not the day of my death.

There is a towering mental demon we have yet to mention: the idea that I will die, but sometime *later.* Not today.

We hide behind the statistics. The statistics say that there is an average lifespan — say, seventy-five years. And I am still younger than that, so I will not die today.

Applied to a single person — applied to you or me — statistics have no meaning. If I'm the one who dies at thirty, to balance several others who die at ninety, then what?

The very things we use to sustain life can kill us anytime: our car, our house, the food we eat. Death respects no order: children die as their parents look on. When the time comes, no amount of money, no medicine, no surgeon can keep us alive.

It's better then if we decide: I will die today. And it will come true. This conclusion forces us to get up and do something about it while we still have time.

83

As They Grasp Our Hand

Jesus passed by the house of a family whose twelve-year-old daughter had died—

> *And he saw the tumult,*
> *and them that wept*
> *and wailed greatly.*

As we walk through a difficult life, we're blessed with a certain amount of support, certain things that comfort us. However hard things get, we have our family and friends to back us up.

The simple act of owning things—a house, a car; the simple act of going to buy something, anything, grounds us somehow, makes us somebody.

On the day we die, all this support is ripped away in a single moment. Friends and family circle the bed, clutching our hands, and still we slip away, alone, naked as the day we were born.

84

The Body Rests upon the Mind

Jesus said,

> *They can kill your body,*
> *but not your soul.*

And so we die. Not a single person can come with us, not a single scrap of the money or possessions we devoted our entire life to acquiring means anything at all to us now.

But does anything go on? Another recent achievement of the Devil: this more sophisticated, enlightened view that we just stop when our body stops. It is sort of like arguing that the driver must be dead because we can see that his car has broken down.

If the mind were just the brain, if the mind rested upon the body in the way a bowl of fruit sits atop a table, then it's true that we'd be gone the day our body died.

But we've already seen that this is not at all the case. *The body rests upon the mind.* Like everything else around us, our body is something that we experience because of seeds that ripen from our deeper memory, from the degree to which we have cared for others in the past.

When the seeds for seeing ourselves in one form wear out, as all seeds do, then they are replaced by other seeds, for other forms. And so we do go on after death.

85

A Greater Freedom

Jesus stops no less than ten times in the New Testament to warn us about hell. Passing it off as a metaphor is again just wishful thinking by an entire culture that tries to pretend that death itself does not exist.

We do go on after death, and how we experience the next step in our lives again depends entirely upon the seeds we have planted in this present life: *upon whether or not we have taken care of the others around us.*

An expecting mother takes a drink of alcohol or smokes a cigarette. A single chain of DNA, at a microscopic level — in a single cell — is damaged. And for the next fifty years another human being must live with a terrible deformation.

It's naïve to think that the consequences of a single twisted seed in the mind would grow any less after we cross into death. And so it's not just death that we seek our freedom from.

86

Grim Reminders of Ourselves

Jesus said

> *I tell you the truth; I tell you truly. You are young; you dress yourself, and you go wherever you please. But soon you will be old, and you will stretch your hands out feebly; others will dress you, and take you where you have no wish to go.*

Whatever freedom we seek from death and what comes after it, we seek the same freedom from the process of aging.

It doesn't come in a day, and we don't notice it while it's coming, although those who see us only every few years certainly do.

Wrinkles slowly stretch across our face. Skin sags, muscles fade. Thinning hair, and the eyes and ears and intellect slowly shutting down.

The gradual descent into a bent and feeble creature that the rest of the world would rather wasn't around to remind them: this too I will be.

87

Things Fall Apart

The apostle James:

> *These things are like a cloud,*
> *which forms for a few minutes,*
> *and then vanishes away.*

To understand both aging and death, we must understand the more general, natural dying of all things.

The end of a thing is inserted into a thing by its beginning. Forces come together to create a thing, and by creating it they draw to an end. Left to themselves, all created things fall apart, even if nothing else comes along to hurry the process.

Our body and our life are no different. Again, they are being produced by how we behave toward others. Each kind act toward others imparts more life. Without a constant, intentional, and massive concern for others, what life we still posses must daily melt away.

88

A Word about Science

You are ten years old. Two of your friends go driving in a car. The car hits another car. One of your friends is killed. The other walks away without a scratch.

You ask your mother, you ask *science,* why your one friend died, and the other didn't.

"Because his head went through the windshield, and the windshield was harder than his head."

"But, Mom, *why* did he go through the windshield?"

"Because he was sitting in front when they hit the other car."

"Yeah, but *why* was he sitting in front?"

"I don't know, he just got in the front, and the other child didn't. Now don't ask silly questions."

Don't ask silly questions. This is the final answer you get from your mother and the final answer we get from science in its current state.

Science in its present stage of development describes helpfully and accurately *how* the process of aging and death occurs. Certain bodily functions begin to decay, which impacts upon other systems, until a certain irreparable threshold is reached. The organism as a whole then shuts down.

No word on *why* the process begins at any particular moment.

In the case of a car accident, the relative resistive capacity of skull material at the point of impact is exceeded by the forces created by the sudden impetus imparted by the collision — which only explains *how* Johnny died, not *why* he died. Not *why* he sat down in the front. Not *why* the other car turned at that precise moment.

A truly comprehensive form of science cannot fail to incorporate these final questions of *why* things happen. Our current state of science is a matchless contribution to society; but it could be so much more, a final and complete explanation of things: an explanation that, because it is complete, could break through even final problems such as aging and death.

In the end, our wondrous art of science will incorporate an ethical element, an element of compassion. Here's how.

Science as we practice it already recognizes the role of perception in how reality operates. That is, we have reached the point where we recognize that *how a subatomic particle behaves is altered by the very act of our observing it.* Science as it stands today sees a sort of standard reality that is changed by our *looking* at it.

This idea approaches the understanding of the deeper memory that survives among our eastern Christian cousins. And this makes for an intriguing possibility. What if it really is true that our perceptions not only *alter* the world around us, but actually *form its very content?*

And what if the content of our perceptions is determined by how well we have taken care of others in the past?

Can you see, can you sense, a sort of new, very advanced form of science? A science that explores, confirms, and then standardizes through that glorious scientific method the precise acts of kindness required, for example, to plant seeds in the deeper memory which would sustain the perception of life indefinitely.

The end of aging, the end of death. Einstein meets Jesus, if you will.

89

Demons Unslain Slay Us

Jesus said to them,

> *I go my way.*
>
> *You shall try to come with me,*
> *but you shall die in your sins.*
>
> *You will not be able to go*
> *where I go.*

On an immediate level, our own negative emotions — the mental demons we fought in the last section of this book — are what kill us.

The killing takes place on that fuzzy border between the body and the mind. The eastern family draws an extraordinary map of the deepest level of our physical bodies. Here the very energy of life itself flows along channels that are subtle shadows of our veins and nerves.

Linked with the energy of life, as it flows throughout us, travel our thoughts, riding the ineffable force of life like a horseman on a horse. As our thoughts turn, the actual essence of our life turns with them.

Whenever we have a strong negative emotion, whenever a mental demon takes hold of our mind, subtle damage is done to the energy within us that sustains our very life. Death is hastened by the mere act of . . . unhappiness.

90

The End of Death

Jesus said, again,

> *I tell you of a truth*
> *that there are some of you*
> *standing here,*
> *who shall not taste of death*
> *before they see*
> *the kingdom of God.*

We know, though, from our understanding of how the deeper memory works, that just thinking positively is not enough to deal with something as big as death. At any given moment, thousands upon thousands of seeds within us are at differing stages of development.

Some are still in the early stages. They're like wet concrete, still easy to change. Other seeds are just about to break out as the next few minutes of our life, and these are like concrete that is nearly hardened.

Unfortunately, our death is one of these seeds.

By now, no one needs to tell us how to kill death. Seeing ourselves die is just another way of looking at the painting: death is not *in* us; it's something we *see* in us. Change the seeds, and we won't *see* it that way—which is to say, it won't *be* that way.

But it's going to take a tremendous amount of work.

91

They Are Not Enough

Jesus said,

> *Except that your righteousness shall exceed that of these others around you, ye shall in no case enter into the kingdom of heaven.*

One thing we must surely understand, or death will have us. Planting seeds this powerful, enough to stop death itself, cannot be done merely by following the Lord's commandment not to kill. Rather we must also protect life, we must preserve life, we must become great masters in the art of nurturing all life, or we have no hope at all.

There is a certain level of morality required by law. If we shoot a man in the chest, we go to jail. There is a higher level of morality required by custom. We won't get locked up for failing to cover our face when we sneeze at dinner, but Aunt Jane sitting down the table from us will certainly start to frown.

The government, our teachers at school, our church, our parents — all have imparted to us various and sometimes conflicting versions of how far we should go to protect life.

They are not enough.

To defeat death, we must examine all we've ever been taught, and make our own decisions about places where we can go further. It must become the purpose of our life, or else our life will surely end, without purpose.

92

The Source of the Strength Required

Jesus said,

Ye are the light of the world.

And so we will have to reach that fine degree of morality where we stop at work and pick a pencil up off the floor, on the remote possibility that someone might slip on it and fall. We stop using a cellphone in our car — even where it's allowed — because we honor and respect life so deeply that we avoid anything close to hurting someone. Still it is not enough.

Next we have to look beyond the limits of our own little world and explore the worlds of others. How can I contribute to the safety and healthy life of everyone in my neighborhood, my city, my state, my country, my planet?

In the end, our own fear of death will not be enough to sustain us. Human beings have an infinite capacity and resourcefulness to make things happen if they really want to. But "me" alone is too small to deserve this kind of effort, and deep inside we know that.

We will not be able to make the required effort until we are doing it for all of us.

93

No Wrinkles

God said,

Let us make man in our image.

What will our body look like if we do defeat death? Are we doomed to life eternal, piling up ever more wrinkles?

When we restrain ourselves meticulously from anything that may harm any living creature; when we go further and reach out to our entire world, seeking ways to assure health and long life to everyone; then special seeds are planted.

The very way that we look at our hand and see something made of mortal flesh and bone is just the same as looking at a painting. We would see infinitely higher beauty if we planted sufficient seeds.

At this point we would look at our hand and see not flesh, but light. The general structure of our seeds means that we will always see ourselves in the general shape of a human — arms, head, and legs — but now we are made of light itself, eternally youthful, the most exquisite thing you can imagine and more.

Don't be afraid sometimes to sit and dream of what you will be like. Go through old paintings of angels or just your favorite fashion magazine for some ideas. There's no reason not to start planning.

94

On Miracles

In the fourth watch of the night, Jesus went unto the disciples in the boat, walking on the sea.

If you think about it, watching our body turn into light is just a variation on miracles in general—such as learning to see water as solid and walking upon it.

Miracles are real. And they're *not* just something that used to happen in the old days of the Bible but not today.

We've described the key a dozen times, but no harm in reminding ourselves. *Wetness* doesn't belong *in* water any more than *greatness* belongs inside your favorite song (which explains why there are actually people who don't consider it a great song).

Even the very quality that defines a thing — the wetness of water—is something whose existence is spewing forth from the seeds of our own deep memory: from the degree to which we have taken care of others.

This means that we ourselves, if we care enough for others, can work the miracles not only of never-ending life, but of anything else as well. The power comes from our unstoppable desire to help others.

95

A Missing Page from the Morning Paper

And after six days Jesus taketh Peter, James, and John his brother, and bringeth them up onto a high mountain apart. And he was transformed before them; and his face did shine as the sun, and his robe was white as light.

One crucial question should be tickling your mind by now: if Jesus taught some method of escaping death — of transforming the body into light itself — then why don't we see any of these people around today? There must be at least a *few* people in the last two thousand years who have succeeded in this practice. Why don't they show themselves to us? One serious article in the morning paper, with a good photo, would help millions of people!

Whatever good seeds it takes to *perform* a miracle, it takes nearly as many to *witness* a miracle. There's an easy example for this.

In any given place, there are multiple worlds going on. Science is exploring this idea, but we don't really need to go any further than our own kitchen.

When we get up and go to make our morning coffee, one world starts in the kitchen: a human world. But as our pet dog walks in, then another world pops up. Two worlds are overlapping in the same space.

Now admittedly there are some parts of the kitchen that the dog and I see the same way. For example, the space has four walls.

But suppose there's a pen lying on the floor (you didn't notice it, or it wouldn't be there for someone to possibly trip on). To our dog, it's just a stick, its only possible value being something to chew on. For us, it's a writing instrument — a potentially very precious tool for reaching out to many other people.

Now who's right in this case? Is that cylinder on the floor a chew toy, or is it a pen? What is it *really?*

You know the answer. It's both, really — or maybe neither. It just depends on who's looking. A dog simply doesn't have the equipment — the seeds — to perceive the cylinder as something to write with. *But that doesn't mean there's no pen on the floor.*

Of course there are people in history who have followed Christ's teachings meticulously and who have already gained eternal life. Jesus himself plainly said that some of his own disciples would reach this goal within their own lifetimes. The fact that we — those of us who have not yet put in the necessary good work — cannot yet see these people is to be expected and almost comforting: if a dog suddenly picked up a pen to write a friend, it would break the rules that make deathlessness possible in the first place.

Only three disciples are good enough to see who Jesus becomes on the mountain. Let us not be left behind.

96

Meaning Lies Not in Words

Jesus said,

You have ears, but you hear not.

Perhaps a final question here: it may be that we ourselves lack sufficient goodness to meet one of these people of light. But why aren't there at least a few believable records or accounts of such people, in all these years?

This goes to a very deep question about the nature of words themselves. If not even water is wet, in and of itself, then the very meaning that words have is also coming from our side. Jesus was perfectly aware of this and repeatedly says in the Gospels that "only those with ears will hear what I am saying." For every person who grasped the point of one of his parables, there must have been dozens who walked away, shaking their heads, complaining that they didn't come to hear a simpleton tell his stories.

It is possible to live in a world teeming with divine beings, it is possible to be surrounded by people trying to tell us how to become a holy being ourselves, and still simply be unaware that the stick on the floor is a pen. How to break through this threshold, how to actually make contact with beings of light, is an important part of the last step we need to have it all. We call it, simply, fulfillment.

SIX

FULFILLMENT

97

Destiny

Jesus said,

> *Be ye therefore perfect,*
> *even as your Father*
> *which is in heaven*
> *is perfect.*

Why were we born? What are we meant to do in this world? Have we truly lived if we only work and eat and die? You know the answer — you feel it, and you always have.

Make-believe films and novels tell us more about ourselves than the newspapers. The plot is always the same. An apparently unbeatable bad guy comes and threatens everybody. And there's one person (that's us), who's actually not so brave or strong, but by some sort of unexpected courage and self-sacrifice manages to save the world.

Why do they keep making movies like this? Because we want it to come true. We *know* it will come true.

We were born to save the world, each one of us. It is our destiny, and the eastern teachings of Jesus help show us how to fulfill this destiny.

98

Infinite

Jesus said,

> *He shall send his angels with a great sound of a trumpet, and they shall gather together his elect from the four winds, from one end of heaven to the other.*

The power of a seed is restricted by the limits of the action that plants it. Doing good only toward our friends or family has one result. Expanding the good to strangers, and even enemies, has a greater result.

But we want to save the whole world. And so the good we do must be infinite.

There's a story in Tibet about the frog who thought that the well he lived in was the entire world. A crow friend disagreed, and to prove his point he carried the frog to the edge of the sea. When the frog laid his eyes on the infinity of water, his head blew up.

We have no such excuse; we know better. The number of stars visible inside one square inch of the sky as viewed through modern telescopes numbers in the tens of thousands. There are countless worlds in the universe, and countless worlds with life upon them.

It is flatly impossible to plant the necessary seeds to save the world if we don't think about how big the world — the universe — really is; and unless we do our good deeds with a clear motivation of wanting to help every living creature in this larger world.

When the deed is infinite, the seed is infinite. It's a trick: you drop a tiny piece of bread on the ground for a sparrow hopping by. You close your eyes and imagine you are feeding every creature in the universe.

And then the day will come.

99

Each and Every Face

And God saw every thing that He had made, and, behold, it was very good.

We make it a pattern prayer, both at church and in every hour of the day, to do everything we do for every living being, seen and unseen. Seeds are planted that are limitless in scope.

And then one day they ripen, in a special moment, even as we pray. With our eyes closed, we gaze directly upon the face of every living creature — not just upon this world, but upon every world there is. All in a single moment. We are glimpsing what we will become, and we are seeing the ones we are doing it for.

Can you imagine what life is like after this one glorious moment?

100

Sliding into Heaven

And their eyes were opened; and they knew he was Jesus; and he vanished out of their sight.

Think carefully. Just how did you expect it to happen? Going to heaven, that is. You start to cross the street, you look up, suddenly a truck is bearing down on you. And a split second later—surrounded by angels in white?

It doesn't usually happen like that. Something as big as heaven isn't built in a day. It comes upon us gradually, because our good work is progressing, gradually. We get signs, indications, that things are going the way they said it would with the seeds, and then this inspires us to try even harder.

Say, for example, we're working on the seeds for financial security.

At first we're not all that convinced by this idea about the deeper memory and seeds and how I treat others coming back to me as my own world. But then again it certainly fits what Jesus taught—just a more detailed way of explaining how good deeds actually work. And so we decide to give it a try, in a small way. We take that 10 percent of our paycheck, set it aside each week for a month, and then go out to find someone who really needs it.

This doesn't mean writing a check for the Red Cross and letting someone else do all the work—and get all the seeds. It means going out ourselves to buy the food, cook it, and serve it to the hungry with our own two hands. A few weeks later, out of the blue, our stingy boss offers us a modest raise.

Hmm. Maybe it's the seeds, maybe just coincidence. But definitely worth exploring. We give more, we put more of our money and our heart into it.

And all of a sudden, six months down the line, Mr. Stingy offers us a major promotion, along with a substantial pay hike and an extra week's vacation.

This is getting serious. We pump more into our giving. Don't do too much too early; let it come naturally, as you see results. Then you won't quit if there's any minor setback or delay — if Jesus appears but suddenly disappears, because our seeds aren't all that strong yet.

Before long you own half the company. This gives you more resources from which to expand your giving. You start going statewide, national, and then international in your charitable projects.

Things go from amazing to downright impossible. People start giving you estates, sending you checks unrequested in the mail.

And your world begins to change. People all around you seem happier, and definitely more prosperous. The world itself is altering, in a major way. Poverty declines noticeably, even in the poorest of countries.

You're beginning to slide into heaven.

101

Meeting Angels

Jesus approaches Mary Magdalene at the tomb and saith unto her: Woman, why weepest thou? Who seekest thou? She, supposing him to be the gardener, saith unto him, Sir, if thou have borne him from here, tell me where thou hast laid him, and I will take him away.

Again Jesus simply replies, "Mary," and then instantly she sees him as her Master.

While the world around us begins its transformation into heaven, so too do the people around us transform into the other inhabitants of heaven. Those who have already passed away are with us again, everyone vibrant and youthful.

Over the course of our life, a certain progression of seeds has ripened within us, and their tracks are still there. Our new level of good deeds — deeds performed on an infinite level, even as we simply cook a meal at home or close a deal at work — revive and transfigure the image of every person we've ever met.

We are surrounded by angels; we see them; they guide us even further. Keep an eye out for the first one you actually recognize. They seem to enjoy posing as waiters or waitresses in small cafés.

102

Meeting God

God called unto him out of the midst of the bush, and said, Moses, Moses. And he said, Here am I.

To meet God face-to-face, we must understand something of his nature. His essence, his core, is the very fact that what we do unto others shall be done unto us. His inner essence is the fact that there is not a single atom of being — physical, mental, or spiritual — which could ever exist in any other manner.

And so in a way God is the blank screen and the laws by which the world appears upon it, combined within a person of infinite compassion and knowledge.

We meet God by contemplating this essence.

Only in complete silence can God be met.

When the silence is enough, when we understand the essence perfectly; when the death and pain of those around us has pushed us far enough to *want* to meet God, then it is done.

103

Reaching Jesus

Again, the Lord said,

> *A new commandment I give unto you,*
> *That ye love one another*
> *as I have loved you.*

Meeting God — and you will — is something of a milestone, because shortly afterward we gain the power to save the world. That is, we *reach* Jesus.

"Reaching Jesus" can have two meanings. One would be to make contact with the Lord. The other would be to reach the abilities of the Lord ourselves: to become like Jesus.

The eastern branch of the Christian family has always taken the final goal as reaching Jesus in *both* these ways. Jesus came into this world to bring us to our final fulfillment, which is nothing less than learning to do what he himself did upon this planet. To save the world. To save the universe.

A funny little question pops up here: how can I save a world that has already been saved? And even if I do save it, what world will there be for the rest of you to save?

Come on. We went through this already. When three people stand and look at a painting, how many different paintings are really there?

104

The Transformation of the Body

Again Jesus said,

> *Where two or three are gathered in my name, there am I in the midst of them.*

And he meant it literally.

It's one thing to live in a body that doesn't have to die; it's quite another thing to live in a body that can save the world — all the worlds there are.

When we try to imagine how Jesus sits in heaven, we're not all that far off. Obviously the Lord possesses some kind of "home body," the body he lives in on a day-to-day basis — the mirror image of his own infinite goodness and seeds.

This body lives in splendor, utter magnificence and beauty. And it lives so on into eternity, for in every moment the Lord undertakes infinite actions to help us — thus "reinvesting" the seeds, continuing his state of perfection even without consciously thinking to do so.

The actions that Jesus undertakes — coming to a world such as ours, bringing this light of understanding to save one more planet — are performed by his other forms: the infinite variety of bodies, equal exactly in number to the individual needs of every living creature in the universe.

105

Emanation

The Second Book of Kings:

And God was seen upon the wings of the wind.

We will share in the body of Christ. We will come to possess these same forms, this same ability to serve others, on all worlds. It is our destiny. We feel it.

If Jesus can appear as a gardener at his tomb, as a stranger on the road who bumps into his two disciples, or even as a crafty fellow selling his slave Thomas, then of course he can (and we will) emanate or show himself in any form needed to help others progress further along the path.

Obviously any member of the clergy, our parents, or one of our teachers — people who have paid us great kindness in our lives, who have shown us great lessons — may actually be Jesus himself.

And it's impossible to deny that perhaps the most helpful lessons in our life have come from those who've hurt us. And so perhaps they are him as well.

Christ comes in even more unexpected forms, forms we can sense only in times of deep emotion — the death of our mother, the loss of love. And then he touches us in the wind, or with the sound of waves at the shore.

Jesus comes in his one classic form, of course, but it would be naïve to think that he does not appear in infinite other forms, as needed. Perhaps one person in our life is actually the Lord; perhaps all of them are.

Just thinking how this is true plants a seed in us to be able to do the same someday. And it makes life a lot more fun.

106

The Transformation of the Mind

From that time forth began Jesus to show unto his disciples how that he must go unto Jerusalem, and suffer many things, and be killed, and be raised again the third day.

One of the miracles that Christ performs over and over — so often that it is rarely counted among his miracles — is to predict exactly what will happen in the future.

For what is "now"? What decides that the present moment is just this moment, and not half this moment, or else a hundred years?

We experience time in the same way that we experience beauty "in" a painting: because it is flowing from us, from the seeds within us, planted by how we care for others.

If we plant seeds that are infinite — if with every small kindness we do, we consciously dedicate it to fulfilling our destiny upon countless worlds, to gaining the bodies of Christ — then the very limitations of space and time are altered; for again, they flow from us.

This gives us a never-ending, unbroken, and direct awareness of what each being in the universe needs; why they need it; and how we will fulfill it, all in every single moment we live. It removes all limitations of where we can *be* in the same moment. The perfect equipment for a servant of the world.

107

What Will You Teach?

Without a parable spoke Jesus not unto them.

When a teacher speaks only in parables, in metaphors, it leaves things open for lots of different interpretations.

There was a large jewelry chain in America with hundreds of stores. One day they took some of the stores in each city and changed their name to a fancy-sounding British name. They moved all their more expensive jewelry to these high-end stores, and kept the cheaper jewelry in the old stores.

Then they did a strange thing. A memo went out to the higher-end stores encouraging them to place newspaper and TV ads in their towns criticizing the company's own lower-end stores in the same town. "Isn't your bride-to-be important enough for a *better* diamond ring?"

At the same time, the low-end stores of this same company were told to put out ads attacking the high-end stores for their higher prices. "Why pay more?"

People in the industry thought it was crazy — stores owned by the same company told to attack each other. But it raised people's awareness and got them taking sides: "I'm not going to waste my money!" versus "I'm going for quality!" And in the end the firm's total sales of jewelry almost doubled.

Don't put it past people like Jesus to engage in this clever type of marketing. He wants us to have the diamond; he's not so worried about how we get it.

Imagine looking down at our world and trying to design the perfect form of Christianity, or religion in general, for everyone down there. One day this is going to be *your* problem! And you might just make the same decision—that your different groups of customers need different kinds of stores, each one leading them a little further up.

108

Ask for Help

We said it in the beginning:

Ask, and it shall be given to you.

We mentioned one form of prayer called "requesting prayer." And we said that it is impossible to undertake the path set forth in this book — it is impossible to have anything, much less have it all — without a living teacher to guide us.

We can use requesting prayer to find this teacher. It sounds corny, but it does work, because it works through planting seeds.

Each night, just after you've put your head down on the pillow and are about to fall off to sleep, imagine that you have placed your head in Christ's lap, in his cupped hands.

His hands are toasty warm, a quiet, soft, golden light. He is smiling down at us, proud of us for undertaking this courageous task: to have it all, for others and ourselves too. He will watch over us as we sleep, and all the next day.

Just as sleep takes you away, utter a tiny prayer: "My Lord loves me. Please come." Then sleep.

Seeds are planted; he will come in just the right way for us. We draw our teachers to ourselves, and they draw us to heaven, to our destiny.

109

A Powerful Force

Jesus said, again,

All things are possible.

A monk in a Tibetan monastery spends some twenty years going through the five great subjects, all from textbooks that were written during the glory years following the arrival of Thomas. It is a difficult and rigorous course, which less than one in ten completes.

The final examinations, which begin years before graduation, are especially daunting. Hundreds of questions flying at you from dozens of examiners, all to be answered from memory, on the spot.

But after all these years — two thousand years after the new wave of love first touched the East — the final question on the final day remains the same:

Will there be an end to the world's pain?

And you stand up, and you call out, "Yes!" And the examiner stands too, and cries back, "Why?" And then with all the might in your lungs you shout back the words, “Because there is a mighty power!”

And a thousand voices begin to cheer for joy because everybody knows what the power is: all things come from taking care of others.

About the Authors

Geshe Michael Roach grew up in All Saints' Church of Phoenix, Arizona. He is an honors graduate of the Department of Religion of Princeton University, where he lived at the Procter Christian Foundation and served as a student member of the committee to revise the cathedral prayer book. He also received the Presidential Scholar medal from the president of the United States.

On the verge of entering the seminary, Michael suddenly lost three members of his family. This led to over twenty years of study in Tibetan monasteries, seeking help to understand pain and death. Discovering the teachings of Jesus that reached Tibet through the apostle Thomas provided a life-saving key.

Michael is the first American to have completed the geshe course of the five great subjects in a Tibetan monastery. He is a founding member of Andin International Diamond, one of Manhattan's most successful firms, and the author of the international bestseller *The Diamond Cutter.* His projects to help Tibetan refugees have saved hundreds of families.

Christie McNally's spiritual journey began at the age of five, when she asked her mother: "What does God look like?" She grew up in Reseda, California, attending St. Monica's Church and Bethel, Trinity, and Notre Dame church schools. She too pursued the question of why people suffer, finally studying in Tibetan and Nepalese monasteries to find this same wisdom descended from Thomas.

Christie is a professor of religious studies and a translator of ancient Tibetan and Sanskrit, whose works have been published by Doubleday/Random House and other firms. She has served as a textual expert for the Asian Classics Input Project and is a popular international speaker on the links between the religions of the world.

As a couple, Michael and Christie over the last ten years have explored the great cities, rare manuscripts, and oral traditions of Jesus and Tibet, which bear witness to the mission of the gentle Thomas to these lands. In 2003, they completed a three-year silent solitary prayer retreat together in the high desert of Arizona.

Finding Out More: Star in the East

It takes time for these new ideas from Christ's eastern family to sink in. Carry this book around, and read perhaps a few small sections every day for a few months; before lunch or breakfast, for example.

There are also more resources for you. A group of people from all over the world, and from many different denominations, has come together to explore more about the ideas in this book. We've created a source for information called Star in the East, or SIE.

If you have any additional questions that come up in your own mind as you read this book; if we can share any practical advice about how to actually apply these ideas to your own life; then feel free to write or email us at the contacts listed below.

If you've been particularly inspired by the book and really want to go deeper — which of course helps everything go a lot faster — then don't feel shy to drop us a note to see about arranging a small talk in your local area. We have a good group of qualified speakers who can speak at a home or a church, or lead a brief weekly course or weekend retreat.

If you're feeling especially adventurous after reading this book, contact us about helping out with our explorative work: you might end up traveling with one of our teams to the ancient libraries of Ladakh or Mongolia, discovering more of what you've read here, for future generations.

None of this is pushy, just fun: we do it for the love of it, and we've been to just about every kind of Christian church you can imagine, from a five-hundred-year-old cathedral in Ireland to a backyard set-up in rural California.

Feel free to contact us. And good luck.

STAR IN THE EAST
www.starintheeast.org

51 Spicer Run
Grand Island, NY 14072
starintheeast@gmail.com